Elsie and Norm's "Macbeth"

A Comedy

John Christopher-Wood

Samuel French – London
New York – Sydney – Toronto – Hollywood

CHARACTERS

Elsie Grimethorpe
Norman Grimethorpe
William

The action of the play takes place in a working-class
North Country home

Time—the present

ELSIE AND NORM'S "MACBETH"

First performed on October 28th, 1977, at the Walcot Village Hall, Walcot St, Bath, with the following cast of characters:

Norman   John Christopher-Wood
Elsie   Barbara Vaughan
William   Ric Jerrom

Directed by Ric Jerrom

A version of the play (on which this Acting Edition is based) opened at the Gateway Theatre, Chester, on September 7th, 1989, with the following cast of characters:

Norman   Gordon Kaye
Elsie   Madge Hindle

Directed by Andy Jordan and Philip Partridge

For Andy Jordan

AUTHOR'S NOTES

Elsie and Norman are a North Country working-class couple in late middle-age. Well, actually, they're quite old, really, but that's no reason for not having a bash at a bit of culture, is it, even if you *have* never done it before? Elsie is less of a fuss-pot than Norman, who fusses a great deal given half a chance, but that doesn't mean she lets Norman always have the last word. But why tell you this? You'll see anyway.

William, of course, is really the stage manager, but he does have an important bit at the end, which I won't tell you about now.

The set is the interior of a working-class North Country home. It has a kitchen area with a cooker and kitcheny things like that, and a living area with sofa, sideboard, dining-table and chairs etc. It is furnished and decorated in the best of taste from MFI and the Kay's catalogue. Probably there's a portrait of Charles and Di and some of those nice ornaments that you can buy in Benidorm. There are doors either side of the set; one from the kitchen, one from the living area. There are several largish houseplants.

At the start of the play, Elsie wears a housecoat and crimplene slacks; Norman shirt-sleeves, braces, slippers. I'll tell you about the other costumes as they come up, OK? Accents used are all variations on North of England, unless otherwise specified.

Now read on . . .

ACT I

Black-out. Clap of thunder. Elsie's voice can be heard. It is shrill and eerie in authentic Shakespearian witch fashion

Elsie   When shall we three meet again
                    In thunder, lightning, or in rain?
                    When the hurly-burly's done,
                    When the battle's lost and won.
                    That will be ere set of sun.
                    Where the place? Upon the heath.
                    There to meet with——

Norm (*off*) Where's me teeth?

The Lights come up to reveal Elsie standing C *holding a copy of "Macbeth"*

Elsie What?

Norm (*off; shouting*) Me teeth! Me teeth, woman! I can't do it without me teeth! What have you done with 'em?

Elsie Have you looked in your pocket?

Norm (*off*) Don't be bloody daft! They're not in me . . . oh.

Elsie Now, where was I? You've gone and interrupted me flow.

Norman enters

Norm All right, all right, I'm sorry. Oh! (*He notices the audience*) You didn't tell me they were here.

Elsie Ooooh, so they are. Hallo! (*She puts her copy of "Macbeth" on the sideboard*)

Norm Hallo. Blimey, there's a lot of 'em. You didn't promise 'em tea and biscuits or anything, did yer?

Elsie No.

Norm Thank God. Well, er, ladies and gentlemen. Good-evening and welcome to number forty-one Laburnum Avenue.

Elsie I hope you've all wiped your feet.

Norm Shut up, Elsie. Well, I expect you're all a bit excited, like, wondering what all this is about. Well, it's like this, you see. Me and Elsie, we got a bit fed up with inviting people of an evening just to play Trivial Pursuit and watch *Dynasty*. Didn't we, Elsie?

Elsie We did.

Norm We did. We began to feel that we was leading an empty and pointless existence.

Elsie We began to feel an unnameable yearning, a yawning gap in our emotional fulfilment, an intellectual abyss that *Dempsey and Makepeace* was unable to fill. Didn't we, love?

Norm That's right. And we realized that what we lacked—indeed what the whole of Laburnum Avenue lacked—was culture.

Elsie Culture.

Norm So, when the mobile library van come round last week, I told 'em to cancel my reservation on *The Rambo Fireside Fitness Book*, and give me summat cultural. Which is how we wound up with this *Macbeth* thing. Now, before you start getting puzzled, I might as well tell you that *Macbeth* is not a new Waddington's game. Is it, love?

Elsie No. It is one of the greatest pieces of literature what has ever been wrote in the English language, by the greatest playwright that has ever lived. Shakespeare.

Norm And that's not Arnold Shakespeare as has the scrapyard next to the off-licence. No. William Shakespeare. Well, anyway, we read this *Macbeth*, me and Elsie, and we thought it were smashing, didn't we?

Elsie Fabulous.

Norm We realized straight away that here was a play of amazing depth and subtlety.

Elsie A masterpiece of poetic and psychological drama, Norman.

Norm Yes. So we decided that we would put it on for you. Mind you, it has its faults—I mean credit where credit's due, it's a rattling good story, but we thought there was one or two things that needed improving, didn't we, Else?

Elsie Yes. Well, for a start off, it's far too long.

Norm It is! I mean, if we were to do it the way William wrote it, we'd still be here after the pubs shut, and there's no sense in that, is there? Now, there's a reason why it's too long, isn't there, Else?

Elsie Too much poetry.

Norm Right! Not that we're against poetry, you understand. In its place. But William, he just gets carried away sometimes. I'll give you a for instance. (*He picks up the copy of "Macbeth" from where Elsie put it down, on the sideboard, and sits next to her on the sofa*) We'll do 'em that bit we were looking at the other day, with the King and Banquo in.

Elsie Shall I be the King?

Norm Yes.

Elsie   King: This castle has a pleasant seat;
                            The air nimbly and sweetly recommends itself
                            Unto our gentle senses.

Norm   Banquo: This guest of summer,
                            The temple-haunting martlet, does approve,
                            By his lov'd mansionry, that the heaven's breath
                            Smells wooingly here: no jutty, frieze,
                            Buttress, nor coign of vantage, but this bird
                            Hath made his pendant bed and procreant cradle:
                            Where they most breed and haunt, I have observed
                            The air is delicate.

See? It's overdone, innit? Now, what that bit should really go like is this:

Elsie Nice castle, this, Banquo.

Norm Ay—good bird-nesting country an' all.

See? Snappier! More punchy! I've actually had to do quite a lot of rewriting, as those of you as are familiar with the play will realize. Not that I should think many of you lot are. I'm quite proud of how it's turned out, though.

Elsie Now, Norman, stop hiding your light under a bushel. Norman is no stranger to the world of literary endeavour. He's had several articles published in the *Pigeon Breeders' Gazette*, haven't you, love?

Norm (*bashfully*) Ay, well, I suppose I have.

Elsie And another thing—there's far too many people.

Norm (*looking at the audience*) Oh, I don't think so. There's a few chairs empty over there. Them ones we got at MFI. (*This line can be adapted according to how full the house is, e.g. if it's packed, "You're right. Shall I tell some of 'em to go home?"; if nearly empty, "You must be bloody joking!" etc.*)

Elsie No, no! Not here! I meant in the play. There's too many people in it.

Norm Oh, ay.

Elsie I mean, there's three witches. What do you need three for?

Norm Probably something to do with the Witches' Union—demarcation, I shouldn't wonder. You know, one for spells, one for potions, one for general cackling. Something like that.

Elsie Anyway, there's far too many. I mean, the way William's wrote it, you'd need a theatre full of actors to do it. You'd hardly be able to do it in a living-room at all.

Norm So what we did was chuck out all them extra characters and just got it down to basics. I mean, likely William only put 'em in in the first place 'cos his Uncle Walter or somesuch wanted a part, an' of course, once he'd given one to Uncle Walter, Auntie Ethel wanted one, and then the steward at the British Legion, and so on. You know how it is. I mean, why else would he write in characters like "A Scottish Doctor"?

Elsie We're not having Uncle Walter in it, are we?

Norm Course not! You know who's in it. There's only us in it. (*He turns to the audience*) Now I know what you're thinking! You're thinking that even with all William's relations thrown out, there's still more than two people in *Macbeth*—and you'd be right!

Elsie You see, we thought if we had other people in it they'd all be fighting over who had most lines, and sulking 'cos they hadn't got the best costume. I know it were like that in the last play I were in.

Norm That were *Romeo and Juliet*, weren't it? At the Hinckley Road School for Girls.

Elsie That's right. I played the first Capulet servant. Mind you, I should have been Romeo if that Nora Sedgewick hadn't smarmed round the teacher, nasty little minx! Anyway, Norman and me decided that to avoid arguments we'd play all the parts, what with our previous theatrical experience and all. Norman were in the Regimental production of *The Rocky Horror Show* when he were in the Territorials, weren't you, love?

Norm That's right.

Elsie So don't be deceived into thinking there's other people in it, because you probably will be, when you're watching it, like, on account of our startling character changes. No, it's just Norman and me, amazing as it may seem.

Norm Well, I think they've got the picture. I think we're about ready to start. We can skip that witch bit at the beginning. They've already heard most of it. You go off and get changed, love, and we'll go on to the next bit.

Elsie exits

During the next speech, Norman removes his trousers and puts on a kilt with braces and a tin hat, Second-World-War style. He also rearranges the furniture to create more acting space, and finally picks up a toy plastic sword

I suppose I should tell you a bit about what's happening at the start of the play. Well, for a kick-off, it's all about Scotland. Stands to reason, doesn't it? If it'd been about England, he'd just have called it *Beth*, wouldn't he? Anyway, King of Scotland's army, that's Duncan, his name is, has just had a bit of a dust-up with the King of Norway and a bloke called Macdonald—don't worry about them, by the way; they get knocked out before they get chance to come on. Handy, really. Anyway, Macbeth's done very well for himself in the fighting. In this first scene I play a soldier. (*Tin hat and sword now*) Actually, William calls him a "Bleeding Captain", but I think the less of that sort of talk the better. (*He strikes a pose*) Right!

Elsie (*off; Scottish accent*) Och ay! It's a braw bricht moonlicht nicht the nicht! Hoots, mon! (*She sings*) "There was a soldier, a Scottish soldier . . ."

Elsie enters, as Duncan. She wears a cardboard crown, a false moustache, and a royal robe which is actually a plaid car blanket. She speaks in a sort of Chic Murray Scots drawl

Norm/Captain	The King of Scotland!
Elsie/Duncan	Now then, our Captain, what's doing today?
	I hear there's been trouble with the King of Norway.
Norm/Captain	There has that, Your Highness, and Macdonald as well,
	But good old Macbeth has been giving 'em Hell!
	Macdonald played lousy, he never scored once,
	'Cos Macbeth caught him offside and cut off his bonce!
	Him and that Banquo, they'd fair make you laugh—
	They were all over Norway, as well, second half.
Elsie/Duncan	D'you mean that we've won, then? Is that what you mean?
Norm/Captain	We have that, Your Highness!
Elsie/Duncan	I must tell the Queen!

Elsie exits

Norm (*removing the tin hat and putting it down*) Now, you'll have noticed that that scene were done in poetry. It's not actually William's poetry, that. I wrote it. Meaning no disrespect to the lad, of course, but his poetry's not up to much. Most of it doesn't even rhyme. Right. Next scene. On the heath!

Norman exits

Elsie enters as the Witch. She wears a pointy hat and is astride a vacuum cleaner. She cackles a lot

Elsie/Witch 'Allo, everybody! These things (*i.e. the vacuum cleaner*) is much better than them old-fashioned brooms, you know—cleaner and much more efficient. And the Speedikleen Medusa here is also exceptionally good value for money. It says so in *Witch*. (*She cackles*) Oooh, I love bein' a witch! I'm really evil! I like pullin' guinea pigs' heads off! (*She cackles*) I like sendin' deaf people record tokens! (*She cackles*) I like puttin' itching powder in suppositories! (*She cackles*) God! I'm so nasty, I even stick pins in pictures of Princess Di! (*She cackles*) Oooh, I'm horrible, and wicked, and vicious, and spiteful, and bad! (*Cackle, cackle, cackle*)

Norm (*off*) Get on with it!

Elsie I'm getting into character, Norman.

Norm (*off*) I'll be getting into me pyjamas if you carry on much longer.

Elsie All right. (*She clears her throat*)

Elsie/Witch   I am the only witch in this play,
        The other two aren't in it.
        I'm waiting for Macbeth to come this way—
        He'll be here in just a minute.
        I've got a few things to say to him,
        And Banquo, for that matter.
        It'll put the wind up the pair of them
        When we have our little natter.

Norman enters as Macbeth. He is wearing a tartan jacket and an over-large tam-o'-shanter. He is carrying Banquo, who is a large toy panda with a kilt. Banquo's voice, throughout the play, is ventriloquized by whoever is holding him, or is nearest to him on stage

Norm/Macbeth   I wish we hadn't come this way.
        I'm fed up to the teeth.
        It's raining bloody cats and dogs.
        I hate this blasted heath!
        Me bunions ache, and I'm soaking wet—
        I'll probably catch me death!
        It were your idea to come out here.

Norm/Banquo   Who's that over there, Macbeth?

Elsie/Witch   Hallo, Macbeth!

Norm/Macbeth   How d'you know my name?

Elsie/Witch   Well, I knew you weren't Harry Lauder.
        I'm the Witch, and that there's Banquo,
        And you're the Thane of Cawdor.

Elsie Now, you're probably wonderin' what that means, Thane of Cawdor. Well, it's Scottish, you see. It means somebody sort of high up—so it's quite something if you get to be the Thane of Cawdor. Similar to being a prefect.

Norm/Macbeth   Don't talk daft, you silly witch!
Your brains must be out of order.
You must have got your names mixed up—
I'm not the Thane of Cawdor.

Elsie/Witch   That's all you know, clever clogs,
And I'll tell you another thing—
I know you don't look up to much,
But you're going to be the King.

Norm/Banquo What about me, then? Am I going to be the King?

Elsie/Witch It's hardly likely, is it, dear? Not looking like that. Face facts. No, you're not. However, I have to tell you that all your kiddies will be kings, though I can't for the life of me see how you're going to manage that. Still, there it is. Ta-ta, then!

The Witch exits, cackling

Norm/Macbeth What d'you make of that then, Banquo?

Norm/Banquo Search me.

Norm/Macbeth Any road up, it looks like I'm going to be King, and you're not. Lads down Dunsinane snooker club'll never believe it!

Norm/Banquo Well. She said all my kiddies is going to be kings. Nur nur na nur nur.

Norm/Macbeth (*hitting Banquo round the head*) Shurrup! Lot of nonsense. She's probably not a witch at all. She's probably from *Game for a Laugh*.

Elsie enters as the Messenger. The Messenger, whether played by Norman or Elsie, wears a postman's hat and one of those glasses, false nose and moustache sets that you get from joke shops. She carries a postbag, and speaks in a very silly voice indeed—a sort of nasal sing-song with cleft palate

Elsie/Messenger   Are you Macbeth?
Norm/Macbeth   That's right, I am.
Elsie/Messenger   I've been looking everywhere!
I've brought a message from the King.
It's registered—sign there!

She proffers a clipboard and pencil. Macbeth signs

The King's right pleased with what you did,
Bashing them Norwegian peasants,
And just to show his gratitude
He's sent you a little present.

She proffers a brown paper parcel. Macbeth accepts it

There's some handkerchiefs, some ties and socks,
And a five-pound postal order.
You can have till Wednesday morning off,
And you're promoted—Thane of Cawdor.

The Messenger exits

Norm/Macbeth Bloody hell! It's true! I *am* the Thane of Cawdor! Wait till I
tell the missis! (*He starts moving off-stage*)

Norm/Banquo What about my kiddies bein' kings, then? Are you going to
tell her about that?

Norm/Macbeth No, Banquo, I'm not! She's not interested in your kids!
She's interested in me!

Norm/Banquo But that's what the Witch said.

Norm/Macbeth (*as they exit*) I know it was! Just stop going on about it, will
yer?

Macbeth and Banquo exit

*Elsie enters as Lady Macbeth. She wears a housecoat not dissimilar from
Elsie's own, except it's tartan. She is reading aloud from a postcard*

Elsie/Lady Macbeth "Dear Mrs Macbeth, Weather is lovely here. Went
swimming with Banquo yesterday. Won the battle with the Norwegians
seven-nil. King was very pleased. Met a witch the other day and she said I
was going to be Thane of Cawdor and then King. What do you think of
that? She also said all Banquo's kids was going to be kings, and he hasn't
stopped going on about it since. And do you know, sure enough, I *have*
been promoted Thane of Cawdor! Makes you think, doesn't it? Mind
you, I don't see how I'm going to be King, not without Duncan and his
little son Malcolm dying suddenly, and that's not very likely. Bye for now.
Wish you were here. Love, your Macbeth. P.S. Unless I killed them, I
suppose, but that's not very nice, is it?" Ooooh! Thane of Cawdor! That's
nice. I suppose I'm the Thaness then. But if he's going to be King, that
means I'll be Queen Macbeth! That's more like it! We'll be able to move
out of this dump, and live in a proper detached palace at Dunsinane.
Actually, I think I'll change it to Dunromin. And we'll have a low-level
avocado toilet suite and room dividers everywhere! Oooh, I can hardly
wait! All he's got to do is kill King Duncan and get Malcolm out of the
way. Mind you, I bet he doesn't want to do it, big soft bugger! I can see
I'm going to have to give him a good talking to when he gets home!

Norman enters as a Messenger

	Aha! It is a messenger! What tidings do you bring?
Norm/Messenger	I've come from Scone, Your Ladyship, with a tele-
gram from the King.
	It says:
	"Have promoted your husband T. of C.,
	Which isn't peanuts, is it?
	And so you can show your gratitude
	We're coming on a visit.
	We don't just want a cup of tea,
	We want a proper boiled-ham spread—
	And we'll likely want to stay the night,
	So better air the bed.
	We'll want a cannon salute as well,

                              Of twenty or thirty shots,
                              And we like our eggs done sunny side up,
                              Signed Duncan, King of Scots."
Elsie/Lady Macbeth   Where's Macbeth, then? He should be here.
                              It doesn't show much loyalty
                              Leaving his wife at home on her own,
                              When we're going to be visited by royalty.
Norm/Messenger   He'll be here at once, Your Ladyship.
                              He's caught the express train.
Elsie/Lady Macbeth   Well, I hope he bought a first-class ticket
                              Now he's been made a Thane.

The Messenger exits

(Overacting wildly, striding about and gesticulating)
                              The raven himself is hoarse
                              That croaks the entrance of Duncan
                              Under my battlements. Come, you spirits
                              That tend on mortal thoughts, unsex me here,
                              And fill me from the crown to the toe, top-full
                              Of direst cruelty! Make thick my blood,
                              Stop up the access and passage to remorse;
                              That no compunctious visitings of nature
                              Shake my feil purpose, nor keep peace between
                              The effect and it! Come to my woman's breasts——

Norm *(off)* Elsie! You can't say that! It's not nice!

Elsie I wish you'd stop interrupting, Norman, when I'm communing with
my public! Anyway, that's the way William wrote it.

Norm *(off)* I don't care! William might be a dirty-minded little devil, but
this is family entertainment! You're a respectably married woman! You
can't go round talking about your breasts in public!

Elsie/Lady Macbeth *(sighing deeply)* ... Come to my woman's ... chest,
                              And take my milk for gall, you murdering ministers,
                              Wherever in your sightless substances
                              You wait on nature's mischief! Come thick night
                              And pall thee in the dunnest smoke of hell,
                              That my keen knife see not the wound it makes,
                              Nor heaven peep through the blanket of the dark
                              To cry, "Hold, hold!"

Norman enters as Macbeth. He gives her a peck on the cheek

Where have you been?

Norm/Macbeth Hallo, dear. I've been up at Scone getting my Thane of
Cawdor diploma. Aren't you proud?

Elsie/Lady Macbeth That's all very well, but the King of Scotland's coming
here tonight, and we haven't a thing in the house. You'll have to run
down the corner shop.

Norm/Macbeth *(crestfallen)* Yes, dear.

Elsie/Lady Macbeth And the spare bed's not been aired, and we haven't any red carpets. I haven't even put the cat in the adage. And then you don't bother to turn up till the last minute.

Norm/Macbeth Sorry, dear.

Elsie/Lady Macbeth And what's this about a witch saying you're going to be King?

Norm/Macbeth That's right.

Elsie/Lady Macbeth Well, that means you'll have to kill Duncan tonight, then, after he's had his tea. I don't see how you're going to be King otherwise.

Norm/Macbeth (*panicked*) Do I have to, dear? I mean it's not very hospitable, is it? I thought maybe we could just, er, wait and see if he pops it. I've heard he's got a bad chest.

Elsie/Lady Macbeth (*sternly*) Macbeth!

Norm/Macbeth Oh . . . well . . . look, let's talk about it later. King'll be here any minute.

Pause, then meaningfully . . .

I *said, King*'ll be *here* any minute!

Elsie (*penny dropping*) Oh! Yes!

Elsie exits in a tearing hurry, to re-enter, breathless, by the other door, as Duncan. She sings "Oh, you tak' the High Road and I'll tak' the Low Road and I'll be at Macbeth's hoose afore ye", from off-stage, to cover the costume change

Norm/Macbeth (*kneeling*) Your Majesty!

Elsie/Duncan	Evening Macbeth, nice castle you've got.
	It's all right, you don't have to kneel.
	I'm worn out with kingin'. Think I'll go straight to bed.
	I shan't be wanting a meal.
	I got the last bus from Balmoral.
	I had to wait two hours at Fife.
	It's enough to make you hang up your crown.
	Oh, by the way, how's the wife?
Norm/Macbeth	She's very well, thank you, Your Highness.
	She's upstairs making the bed.
	Will you want some black pudding for breakfast,
	Or will you have porridge instead?
Elsie/Duncan	No thanks, I'll lie in in the morning—
	I don't want to get up before eight.
	Let's hope there's no murder plots, eh, Macbeth,
	Or else I'll be lying in state!
	Ha, ha!

Duncan nudges Macbeth in the ribs, and exits

Norm/Macbeth Ha ha. (*He turns to follow Duncan's exit with his eyes, then turns back to the audience with a manic murderous expression. He overacts* *wildly during the next speech, grimacing and gesticulating madly. The gestures tend to be over-literal and pantomimic, e.g. when he says the word "jump" he jumps in the air, etc.)*

> If it were done when 'tis done, then 'twere well
> It were done quickly: if the assassination
> Could trammel up the consequence, and catch,
> With his surcease, success; that but this blow
> Might be the be-all and end-all here,
> But here, upon this bank and shoal of time,
> We'd jump the life to come. But in these cases
> We still have judgement here; that we but teach
> Bloody instructions, which, being taught, return
> To plague the inventor: this even-handed justice
> Commends the ingredients of our poisoned chalice
> To our own lips ...

Norm Where does William get this stuff from?

Elsie enters as Lady Macbeth

Elsie/Lady Macbeth Well, have you done it yet?

Norm/Macbeth What?

Elsie/Lady Macbeth Have you done him in? Duncan? I've already started writin' the invitations to our Coronation do.

Norm/Macbeth No. I haven't. I don't think we should do it. It's too risky. His little lad Malcolm's going to be here soon, and Banquo, and that Macduff.

Elsie/Lady Macbeth All the more reason for getting on with it, then, yer big girl's blouse! What's the matter with you?

Norm/Macbeth It's not right! After all, he's been nice enough to us, making me a Thane and all.

Elsie/Lady Macbeth (*exasperated*) Look, do you want to be King or don't you?

Norm/Macbeth Supposin' he wakes up?

Elsie/Lady Macbeth He won't wake up. I put Valium in his cocoa.

Norm/Macbeth (*groaning with reluctance*) Oh ... I don't want to do it! (*Sudden inspiration*) Anyway, I can't do it. I've just remembered. I've got to take me library books back. (*He makes to exit*)

Elsie/Lady Macbeth Typical! Just typical! It were the same with that chicken last Christmas.

Norm/Macbeth (*stung*) Trust you to bring that up!

Elsie/Lady Macbeth "Don't let's be payin' butcher's prices for turkey," you said. "Daylight robbery," you said. "Let's be sensible and raise our own Christmas dinner."

Norm/Macbeth (*defensively*) Well, it seemed like good idea at the time.

Elsie/Lady Macbeth So you bought that scrawny horrible little chicken. Cost us a fortune to feed the little horror.

Norm/Macbeth Don't talk like that about our Timmy!

Elsie/Lady Macbeth And what happened! Come Christmas Eve you wouldn't kill it.

Norm/Macbeth Well. It were the way he looked at me. He were more like one of the family.

Elsie/Lady Macbeth Hangin' a stocking full of chicken feed on the hen run! And we had to have flippin' corned beef sandwiches for Christmas dinner!

Norm/Macbeth Well, you wouldn't kill him, either!

Elsie/Lady Macbeth It's not my job! Who wears the trousers in this house?

Norman looks at his kilt, looks at Elsie's slacks, looks at the audience

That's not the point! Either you do Duncan in tonight, and sharpish, or I'm going home to Mother! And you can wipe that smirk off your face, because I'll be taking our Leeds Liquid Gold account book with me!

Norm/Macbeth All right! All right! I'll do it! I'll do it! (*He moves towards the kitchen exit*)

> Is this the breadknife I see before me,
> The handle towards my hand?
> Or have me eyes gone funny?
> It might be swollen glands.
> Must I go forth and do the deed?
> Must I do him to death?
> (*Wheedling*) Couldn't I do it tomorrow?

Elsie/Lady Macbeth Oh, hurry up, Macbeth!

Macbeth exits. Enormous bashing, crashing and shrieking from off stage. Macbeth re-enters looking serious

Norm/Macbeth I have done the deed! (*He produces a dead chicken from behind his back*)

Elsie/Lady Macbeth (*wailing*) Timmy! (*She faints*)

Norman puts the chicken in the oven, and moves over to sit on the sofa. Elsie joins him

Norm Now, you've probably been wondering why there's been no what you might call comic relief in this play. It's very serious stuff, you're thinking. Well, there's a reason for that, isn't there, Elsie?

Elsie It's his jokes.

Norm Now there you've hit it. His jokes. Now, there's supposed to be comic bits in *Macbeth*. I say there's supposed to be—if it weren't for our William's sense of humour. (*He picks up and opens the copy of "Macbeth"*) Listen to this: this is supposed to be a joke ... (*He reads*) "Faith, here's an equivocator that could swear in both the scales against either scale, who committed treason enough for God's sake, yet could not equivocate to Heaven. Oh, come in, equivocator." (*He looks helpless*) Well, I mean who'd laugh at that? But as I said to Elsie, that's our William all over. I said that to you, didn't I? That's William all over.

Elsie William?

Norm Shakespeare.

Elsie Arnold Shakespeare, you mean? Who has the scrapyard next to the off-licence?

Norm Not Arnold! (*He waves the book at her*) William. William!

Elsie Oh, yes.

Norm So we had to throw out all William's jokes. Honestly, they wouldn't have made anybody laugh. There's some *worse* than that! I did think of writing some funny bits in, but . . . well, to be honest with you, I'm more what you'd call a serious writer. So I'm afraid it's just going to have to carry on being a bit gloomy, like, right till the end. Still, it is a tragedy, after all, and culture's culture, isn't it? (*To Elsie*) Right, then. Let's get on with it!

Elsie exits. There is the sound of door chimes

Norm/Macbeth   (*striking a pose*) Who knocks upon my castle door?
I bet it's the police!
I wish I'd never done it now—
I'll get ten years, at least!
They haven't abolished hangin' yet—
I'll wind up on Death Row!
Come on then, put the bracelets on!

He shuts his eyes and extends his wrists, as . . .

Elsie enters as Lady Macbeth, carrying Banquo and Fleance, his son, a smaller toy panda in a kilt

Oh, it's you, Banquo.

Elsie/Lady Macbeth My Lord, the right noble Banquo, destroyer of Norway, general of the King's armies, well-beloved of his Majesty——

Norm/Macbeth Yes, yes, yes. What is it, Banquo?

Elsie/Banquo   I've come to see his Majesty.
I heard he was here tonight,
So I thought I'd come and stay for tea,
If that'll be all right.

Norm/Macbeth   Well, if you think you have to,
I daresay we can find a bun.
Will it be for two of you?
Who's the little furry one?

Elsie/Banquo   How's that prophecy coming along,
The one the Witch said to you—
About you going to be the King?
You don't believe it, do you?
She said my family's going to be kings . . .

Norm/Macbeth   Yes, I know about all that!
Get back to the point, will you,
Who's the little brat?

Elsie/Banquo   Well, I've heard another prophecy—
I've just been to a seance—
And they're going to name police cars after us.
Oh, this is my son Fleance.

Norm/Macbeth Hallo.

Elsie/Banquo Say hallo to Mr Macbeth, Fleance.

Elsie/Fleance Shan't!

Elsie hits him with Banquo

Hallo.

Norm/Macbeth Well, if you're stopping, I might as well show you to your
cage ... er ... chamber. Come on, then. (*He takes Banquo and Fleance
from Elsie*)

Norm/Banquo D'you think it's true, then, about my family being Royalty?

Norm/Macbeth (*despairing*) Oh, God!

Macbeth exits, with Banquo and Fleance

Elsie/Lady Macbeth Well! So far, so good. Assuming Duncan's out of the
way, that just leaves Malcolm, his son, next in line—so he'll have to go,
too. Shouldn't be too much trouble—he's only little. Still, I expect
Macbeth'll be too soft to do it. He's got no ambition, he hasn't. No get up
and go. If I left it up to him, he'd probably settle for a new allotment
instead of being King of Scotland. Well, he'll have to change! I want them
tiaras and ermine twin-sets! I want to be a Royal! I want me picture in
Woman's Own! And I'm not going to let a little bit of murderin' stand in
my way!

*Norman enters as Malcolm, who is a twelve-year-old schoolboy. He wears a
school blazer and cap over his kilt, and talks in a breathless prep school
voice, Terry Scott fashion*

Norm/Malcolm Hallo! I'm looking for my dad. Is my dad here? You seen
my dad?

Elsie/Lady Macbeth Ah. It's little Prince Malcolm, isn't it?

Norm/Malcolm S'right. I'm lookin' for my dad. He's supposed to be stayin'
here. 'Ere, you Mrs Macbeth?

Elsie/Lady Macbeth Yes, love, that's right. Do come and have a sit down.

She pulls him over to the sofa. They sit

Norm/Malcolm Want my dad! He owes me three weeks' pocket money, and
I gotta pay off my marbles debts, else Fatty Smithson'll smash me up.
You gotta glass of water?

Elsie/Lady Macbeth Of course, love. I'll get you one straight away. (*She
goes to the kitchen, which is behind the sofa, and fills a glass from a large
bottle of Domestos*) Here, drink it all up! You must be thirsty.

Norm/Malcolm No, I just want it to keep my tadpoles in. (*He takes
"tadpoles" from his pocket and drops them in the glass*) Oh! Looks like
they're dead! Wotta swindle! I gave three conkers for them, too. Where's
my dad, then?

Elsie/Lady Macbeth Oh, ah ... he's asleep. Won't be able to see him till the
morning. (*She starts to creep up behind him, hands outstretched, obviously
intending to strangle him*)

Norm/Malcolm Oh cripes! That means no fag money today! What a rotten
swizz!

He turns round, just as Lady Macbeth's hands are about to close on his neck

You haven't got a roll-up, have you?

Elsie/Lady Macbeth (*whipping her hands behind her back*) Aren't you a little bit young to smoke, dear? (*She moves to the sideboard, and rolls up a stick of dynamite in a large cigarette paper, then dons the tin hat*)

Norm/Malcolm Course not! I'm nearly twelve! Anyway, that's nothing. Binns Minor drinks three bottles of gin and Ribena a day, and he's only nine. Most of the third form are on crack. (*He accepts the proffered "roll-up"*) Ta. Bit big, innit, for a roll-up?

Elsie/Lady Macbeth Er ... well, don't forget you're Royalty, dear. You wouldn't want an ordinary one like the common people smoke. (*She holds out the flame of a cigarette lighter, shutting her eyes, and putting a finger in her ear*) Light?

Norm/Malcolm No, ta. I think I'll save it and smoke it with Eddie Windsor in Two B after lights out.

He turns away to put the "roll-up" in his pocket. Lady Macbeth raises the tin hat to brain him with it. He turns round just in time

Coo! (*He grabs the tin hat*) Is that a real steel helmet? Can I wear it? (*He puts it on*) My dad won't let me have one. Are you sure he's asleep?

Elsie/Lady Macbeth I think so.

Norm/Malcolm Couldn't I wake him up?

Elsie/Lady Macbeth I doubt it.

Norm/Malcolm Oh, cheese! (*He turns to the audience*) I wish I was King instead of him.

Lady Macbeth produces a doll dressed as Malcolm, and a large hat pin

I will be, you know, when he's dead. Then I won't have to ask for pocket money any more.

She stabs the doll's leg. Malcolm grabs his leg

Ow!

Lady Macbeth smiles evilly

An' I can have Mars bars whenever I want.

She stabs the doll's bum. Malcolm grabs his bum

Ow!

Even broader smile

Coo, that's a point!

He turns to Lady Macbeth, who is just about to deliver the coup de grâce *to the heart*

You don't think he's died in his sleep, do you?

Elsie/Lady Macbeth (*whipping doll and pin behind her back*) Of course not! Ha ha. What a thing to say!

Norm/Malcolm Couldn't I just have a look?

Malcolm exits, followed at the double by the infuriated Lady Macbeth. There is a huge crash from off-stage

(*Off*) Did you see that? That great big battleaxe just missed me. It must have fallen off the wall. You should get that fixed.

Elsie/Lady Macbeth (*off; containing hysteria*) Yes ... I'll get a man in in the morning.

Several loud pistol shots. A pause

Norm/Malcolm (*off*) Was that a motor bike back-firin'? Coo, look, there's holes in your plaster. You should get that fixed, too.

A howl of frustrated despair from Lady Macbeth

Norman enters as Macbeth

Norm/Macbeth Name police cars after 'em? Banquo cars? He's off his rocker! " 'Ere, Sarge, there's been a robbery down West Street. I've sent PC Hawkins in the Fleance." What is he talking about?

Elsie enters as Macduff. He has a large false beard, tweed jacket, deerstalker hat and pipe. He has a gruff, bluff and hearty voice

(*Without enthusiasm*) Oh, hallo Macduff.

Elsie/Macduff All hail, Macbeth! Is it true the King resideth here this night?
Norm/Macbeth Ay.
Elsie/Macduff And the noble Banquo, destroyer of Norway, general of the King's armies, well-beloved of his m——
Norm/Macbeth Yes, yes, he's here too.
Elsie/Macduff 'Tis said there is a prophecy that Banquo's line shall be invested with kingly puissance and power of——
Norm/Macbeth (*exasperated*) Yes! I had heard! What do you want?
Elsie/Macduff Is the King stirring, worthy Thane?
Norm/Macbeth Er, not yet.
Elsie/Macduff   He did command me to call timely on him.
                     I have almost slipped the hour.
                     I just want to take him his pools coupon,
                     And then I'll have a shower.

Macduff exits

Norm/Macbeth   Ha! the only pools he'll get out there
                     'll be when he wets his pants!
                     Horace Batchelor couldn't help Duncan now—
                     He's had his Treble Chance!

A loud scream off. Macduff enters, wailing

Elsie/Macduff The King of Scotland's dead! Someone's wrung his neck!
Norm/Macbeth (*wildly overacted pretence of grief*) What? Dead! Never! He can't be! God, this is awful! Oh dear, oh dear, oh dear! Oh, what a terrible thing to happen! Poor old Duncan! Oh, woe is me! What are things coming to? Duncan murdered! There's no law and order left! Bring back

the cat! Oh, God, oh God, oh God, oh God! . . . Who's going to be King now, then?

Elsie/Macduff But who can have done so foul a deed?

Norm/Macbeth Search me.

Elsie (*to the audience*) Now, I know what you're thinking. It's obvious to anybody who's done it. I mean, if William'd had Bergerac in his play, he'd have had that one solved before the adverts. Still, that's the way William wrote it, and you can't muck about with great works of literature, can you? But if you think it's a bit daft, I want you to know that it's not our fault.

Elsie/Macduff Approach then the chamber, and destroy your sight with a new Gorgon. Do not bid me speak.

Norm/Macbeth Eh?

Elsie/Macduff Go and have a look at him.

Norm/Macbeth Oh.

Macbeth exits

Elsie/Macduff I fear me Macbeth knows more than he says.
Methinks I smell a rat.
Duncan's foul murder cuts me to the heart—
What with me being loyal and that.

Macduff exits

Norman enters as Malcolm

Norm/Malcolm Cor! I was right! My dad has been done in! And he never gave me my pocket money. What a swizz! I think it was that Macbeth that done it. Yeah! And I bet he wants to do me in next. Well, just let him try, that's all! I'll zap him with my death-ray laser! (*He points defiantly, using his finger as a "gun", then looks at it doubtfully*) P'raps not. Maybe I'll just run away instead. To England. Yeah! (*He looks at his kilt*) I can wear proper trousers there, *and* I won't have to go back to smelly Gordonstoun! All that canoeing and kingin' lessons. I hate it!

Malcolm exits, after leaving a hastily scribbled note on the table

Elsie enters as Macduff, carrying Banquo. They sit on the sofa

Elsie/Macduff Ay, Banquo, there has been bitter work done this night. Duncan foully slain, in circumstances most mysterious, and none do know who did the deed. Hast heard aught that may point us to the murderer? What's that thou sayest? (*Putting an ear to Banquo's mouth*) Yes, I had heard about your descendents being kings, but I don't see what——

Norman enters as Macbeth, carrying a large knife

Norm/Macbeth Well, you're right. He's dead. Pity, that. Haven't seen Malcolm anywhere, have you? I want to break his neck . . . break the terrible news to him. Hallo, what's this? (*He picks up the note from the table and reads*) "Dear All. Have gone to England. Yar boo sucks. Malcolm." Well. There we are, then. That's it, then.

Elsie/Macduff What's what then?

Norm/Macbeth There's your killer! Little Malcolm's done his dad in, nasty little devil, no doubt because he wants to be King—and now he's run away to England 'cos he can't live with his guilt.

Norm (*to the audience*) Well, yes, I know it's pretty feeble, everybody, but it's not my fault if William Shakespeare knows bugger-all about writing thrillers, is it? You know, I sometimes wonder how he ever got the job as World's Greatest Playwright. Frankly, I'm surprised he got as far as the interview.

Norm/Macbeth Well. It's obvious Malcolm's not fit to be King. So who is, then? Eh? What d'you think? (*It is clear who Macbeth thinks it should be*)

Elsie/Macduff In sooth, one of Duncan's trusty lieutenants, proven in battle, must now take the throne——

Macbeth is nodding and smiling in agreement

—the which signifies either Banquo——

Macbeth grabs him by the throat and threatens him with the knife

—or you, (*kneeling*) My Liege!

Norm/Macbeth (*realization of what this signifies slowly registering on his face; leaping in the air*) Made it! Yippeeeeee! I'm the King! Ha-haaaa! I've done it, I've done it, I've done it! King! I'll be rich! I'll be famous! Lots of fancy clothes and women! Oooooh, I can kill anybody I don't like! Power at last! I'm the King! I'm the King! (*Singing*) Here we go, here we go, here we go!

Macbeth exits, dancing

Elsie/Macduff   I'm not quite sure he's the man for the job.
I hope I did the right thing.
He doesn't seem quite mature enough
To make a really satisfactory King.
It may not be safe around here now—
I'd be better off in Fife.
I'll not hang around to see him crowned—
I'm off home to the wife.

Macduff exits

Norman enters as Macbeth, now wearing the crown and royal robe

Norm/Macbeth Well, then, now I'm the King, I think we ought to have a bit of a knees-up to celebrate, like. A proper do, with crates of brown ale and lots of potted meat sandwiches. I must get the missis on to it. Where is she? (*Calling*) Come on, everybody, we're having a banquet!

No response

Everybody? Macduff? I said WE'RE HAVING A BANQUET!

Norm/Banquo (*who is still on the sofa, remember?*) Did you call?

Norm/Macbeth Banquet, I said! Banquet! Not Banquo!

Norm/Banquo Well, you've done very well, haven't you? You're the King
now.

Norm/Macbeth Ay. And you'd better not forget it.

Norm/Banquo Just like the Witch said.

Norm/Macbeth Just like the Witch said.

Norm/Banquo So if she was right about you, maybe she was right about me.
When do you think my lot are going to start being kings, then?

Norm/Macbeth (*grabbing him by the throat in a fury*) Look, Banquo, why
don't you take Fleance and go and play Blind Man's Buff on the cliff-top
for a bit. I'm busy! (*He hurls Banquo off stage*) Banquo! Banquo? I'm sick
to death of hearing about bloody Banquo! "What a nice chap Banquo is!"
"Hasn't he done well!" "All Banquo's kids is going to be kings." Smug
little black and white bastard! I hate 'im! He's not even bloody human!
He's just a stuffed bloody panda! Banquo! I'll show bloody Banquo! (*He
blows a police whistle which he is wearing round his neck*)

*Elsie enters as the Murderer. The Murderer wears a black mask and a black
and red striped jumper. He talks in a very deep, very slow, very stupid, sub-
Arthur Mullard sort of voice*

Elsie/Murderer Yus, King?

Norm/Macbeth (*slowly and with heavy emphasis, as if to a small child*) Now,
you know who Banquo is, don't you?

Elsie/Murderer Yus, King. He's the little fat one with the fur.

Norm/Macbeth That's right. Well, Banquo's been very naughty. He's said
bad things about Kingy-wingy.

Elsie/Murderer Oh, bad Banquo.

Norm/Macbeth And Kingy-wingy is very cross with naughty Banquo, and
Banquo's son, Fleance. He is very upset by what they've said about him.

Elsie/Murderer Oh, bad Fleance. Bad, bad Banquo.

Norm/Macbeth And Kingy wants bad Fleance and bad Banquo punished
for all the bad things they've said. So that they won't be naughty again.
Ever! Now, do you understand what you've got to do?

Elsie/Murderer Yus, King. I fix 'em good! Bad, bad boys.

The Murderer exits shaking his head at the wickedness of the Banquo family

Norm/Macbeth　　　　　　I hope all this killing's going to work out right.
　　　　　　　　　　　　I hope I did the sensible thing.
　　　　　　　　　　　　They won't be able to arrest me, will they,
　　　　　　　　　　　　Now that I'm the King?
　　　　　　　　　　　　If they could, I'd be buggered and no mistake!
　　　　　　　　　　　　Trial'd be a sensation!
　　　　　　　　　　　　Killin' Duncan and Banquo and Fleance, too —
　　　　　　　　　　　　It'd be more than just probation!

Elsie enters as Lady Macbeth

Elsie/Lady Macbeth　　How now, My Lord! Why do you keep alone,
　　　　　　　　　　　　Of sorriest fancies your companions making?
　　　　　　　　　　　　Using those thoughts which should indeed have died

With them they think on? Things without all remedy
Should be without regard. What's done is done.

Norm/Macbeth Stop harpin' on, will you, woman! I'm perfectly all right!
Look, you'd best be getting in the kitchen—we're throwin' a party
tonight.

Elsie/Lady Macbeth Oooooh, are we? Who's coming?

Norm/Macbeth Oh ... everybody.

Elsie/Lady Macbeth Well, I'd best get started, then. It's just typical of you
not to tell me till the last minute. I suppose them Banquos'll be wantin'
special food, an' all. What sort of stuff do they eat?

Norm/Macbeth Oh, I shouldn't worry about them. They'll not be coming.

Elsie/Lady Macbeth Why not?

Norm/Macbeth (*shouting*) Never mind why not! They're not coming, that's
all!

Elsie/Lady Macbeth All right, no need to go on. Oooooh! A party!

Norm/Macbeth That's right. A royal banquet.

Elsie/Lady Macbeth In honour of you and me bein' King and Queen. Isn't
it excitin'? It's sort of like a second honeymoon. D'you remember on our
honeymoon what you did that night under the pier at St Andrews?

Norm/Macbeth (*apprehensively*) Mmmm.

Elsie/Lady Macbeth I bet you couldn't do that again, could you? Naughty
boy!

She leads him out by the arm, coquettishly. Giggles off

*Norman enters, carrying Banquo and Fleance. He sits them on the sofa, and
"operates" them from concealment behind it*

Norm/Banquo Lovely day, Fleance.

Norm/Fleance Yes, Dad.

Norm/Banquo Mind you, it'll be rain tonight, I shouldn't wonder.

Norm/Fleance Yes, Dad.

Norm/Banquo Er ... Fleance. Now that you're growing up, there's a few
things I think I ought to tell you.

Norm/Fleance Yes, Dad?

Norm/Banquo A few facts ... er ... about ... er ... life.

Norm/Fleance Yes, Dad?

Norm/Banquo Well, let me see. Well first of all, there's birds, Fleance, and
then there's ... er ... bees ...

Norm/Fleance Yes, Dad.

Norm/Banquo And ... there's pandas.

Norm/Fleance Yes, Dad.

Norm/Banquo (*irritably*) Stop saying, "Yes, Dad," all the time, will you!

Norm/Fleance Yes, Dad.

Banquo hits him. Fleance squeals

Norm/Banquo And pandas have to have little pandas ... like you, son ...
and how that's done is ... er ... I'm not going too fast for you, am I?

Norm/Fleance No, Dad. But if you want to talk about screwing, I wish
you'd hurry up.

Norm/Banquo What?

Elsie enters as the Murderer

Elsie/Murderer 'Ullo. You've been bad boys. You've been so bad I can hardly bear to think about how bad you've been. I'm going to have to kill you for being so bad.

Norm/Banquo Varlet! Caitiff cur! What treachery means this? Who hath bribed thee to essay this deed of vileness? Whoreson slave, it shall be thy last deed upon this earth! For thou com'st against Banquo himself, thrice valiant warrior of the armies of Scotland! Stand thy ground, cur, and be slain!

Elsie/Murderer Get stuffed, Chi-Chi! (*He shoots him*)

Norm/Banquo Oh treachery! Fly, good Fleance, fly, fly, fly!

Norman throws Fleance "flying" off stage, and exits

Elsie/Murderer (*to the "dead" Banquo*) You shouldn't ought to have been so bad. (*He carries him to the door, and throws him out*)

Norman enters as Macbeth

Norm/Macbeth Well? Did you get him? Banquo? The big one? Did you?

Elsie/Murderer Yus, King. Did I do good?

Norm/Macbeth Yes, yes, good boy, good boy! Did you get the little one, too?

Elsie/Murderer Yes. Er . . . no. He got away. I couldn't catch him. You're not going to be cross with me, are you?

Norm/Macbeth Bollocks! Got away! But how! (*He narrows his eyes*) He didn't escape in a police car, did he?

Elsie/Murderer What?

Norm/Macbeth Oh, nothing.

> Then comes my fit again: I had else been perfect—
> Whole as the marble, founded as the rock,
> As broad and general as the casing air—
> But now I am cabin'd, cribbed, confined, bound in
> To saucy doubts and fears . . .

Norm Oh, I'm worn out with all this blank verse! (*He collapses on the sofa*) I think it must be time for the interval, isn't it, Elsie? I'm dying for a cup of tea. Doin' all this Shakespearin' fair makes me throat dry.

Elsie Shakespearin'? Scrap-dealing you mean? I didn't know you had been.

Norm (*shouting*) Not scrap-dealin'! Not Arnold bloody Shakespeare! How many times? William! William Shakespeare! As writes plays! Arnold deals the bloody scrap, William writes the plays!

Elsie (*huffily*) Sorry I spoke, I'm sure.

Norm (*calming down with difficulty*) Anyway, we're having a bit of a break now, everybody. No doubt you'll be wantin' to ponder a bit on all these insights into the Human Condition that a play of this depth gives you. Course you will. It's very tirin' watching great drama. Sorry we haven't enough tea and biscuits for everybody, but I'm sure you can make your own arrangements. See you in about twenty minutes.

Norman and Elsie exit, arguing

CURTAIN

*   *   *

During the interval, Norman and Elsie re-set the stage for Act II, tidying up, setting the dining-table for the "banquet", stirring pans on the cooker, etc., ad-libbing with each other and any of the audience still remaining

*   *   *

ACT II

As the audience come back in for the second act, Norman, as Macbeth, is sitting sulkily at the table. Elsie, as Lady Macbeth, now wearing her own diamante crown and frilly nylon royal robe, is at the cooker, serving out beans on to plates. She plonks a plate of beans on toast in front of Macbeth, takes her place at table and eats her beans contentedly. Macbeth stares at his plate in disgust

Norm/Macbeth Great banquet this turned out to be!

Lady Macbeth blows one of those things that you get at parties—you know, the ones with a feather on that uncurl as you blow them and make a squawking noise

Are you sure you sent the invitations?

Elsie/Lady Macbeth Course I did. Lovely they were, too. Printed on little powder blue cards—"Dear So-and-so," they said, "You are invited to a knife and fork banquet on the occasion of Mr and Mrs Macbeth becoming King and Queen. Tiaras must be worn. Bring a bottle. Rizzvup."

Norm/Macbeth Rizzvup?

Elsie/Lady Macbeth It always says that on proper invitations: RSVP—rizzvup.

Norm/Macbeth (*despairingly*) Oh, God!

Elsie/Lady Macbeth And a little crown at the top with our family motto underneath.

Norm/Macbeth I didn't know we had a family motto.

Elsie/Lady Macbeth Well, I thought we should have, now that we're Royal. So I made one up.

Norm/Macbeth Well, what is it?

Elsie/Lady Macbeth "Glasgow belongs to me."

Macbeth groans in despair

Well, it does, doesn't it?

Norm/Macbeth Bloody hell! Have I murdered half of bloody Scotland for this? Just so we can sit eating beans on toast all on our tod? Beans on bloody toast! Christ, woman, couldn't you do any better than that?

Elsie/Lady Macbeth It was all we had in, and I couldn't get anything from the shops, 'cos they're all shut.

Norm/Macbeth Shut?

Elsie/Lady Macbeth For the coronation.

Norm/Macbeth Aaaagh! Where's Macduff, then? He knows we're havin' a do.

Elsie/Lady Macbeth He left a note saying he was sorry, but he had to go to the dentist.

Norm/Macbeth Sorry, is he? Sorry? He's up to no good, is that Macduff, you mark my words. I'll make him sorry if I get my hands on him.

Elsie/Lady Macbeth Banquo hasn't turned up either.

Norm/Macbeth (*grinning horribly*) No. That's one thing to be thankful for. He won't be showing his furry face round here any more.

Elsie/Lady Macbeth Why not?

Norm/Macbeth 'Cos he's dead, that's why! Done in! Had the stuffing knocked out of him! Heh, heh, heh!

Elsie produces "Banquo's Ghost", i.e. the panda with a ghostly sheet over it. The sheet is tailored to fit over its ears, and looks really ludicrous, believe you me. She sits him in a vacant chair, then carries on eating, as Lady Macbeth, as if nothing had happened

AAAAAAAAAAAAAAAAAAAAAH! (*He runs away and cowers behind the sofa*)

Elsie/Lady Macbeth Whatever's the matter, love? You look like you've seen a ghost.

Norm/Macbeth It's 'im! It's 'im! He's come to get me! He's come to carry me off with him to the great zoo in the sky!

Elsie/Lady Macbeth (*replacing the panda under the table*) Who is, dear?

Norm/Macbeth (*raising his head and pointing*) Him! . . . Oh.

Elsie/Lady Macbeth Are you all right, dear? You're not having one of your turns, are you? You look peaky.

Norm/Macbeth (*returning shakily to the table*) No, no. I'm all right now. You know, I thought for a minute Banquo were sat sittin' there, starin' at me with his little beady glass eyes, as if to say, "Macbeth, you've had it! You may be King, but you'll never make Jubilee Year!" Silly, really.

Elsie/Lady Macbeth Course it is. There's nobody here but us. You were moaning about it a minute ago. I think you ought to take some of your tablets. (*She proffers the bottle*)

Norm/Macbeth No, no, I tell you it's passed off now. Fancy getting upset about that furry little runt! Specially when he's dead! Huh! Going to name police cars after his lot! Ha ha ha! Bloody idiot!

Elsie/Lady Macbeth Can you imagine? Panda cars! Ha ha ha!

Norm/Macbeth (*hysterical mirth*) Who'd give a cop car a daft name like that, eh? Ha ha ha!

Elsie produces Banquo's ghost again

AAAAAAAAAAAAAAAAAAAAH! Gerrout of it! Leave me alone! I'm sorry I did it! I'm sorry, I'm sorry, I'm sorry! I'll give all me money to Animal Lib! Anything! Just go away! Bugger off! (*He cowers behind the sofa, madly swallowing pills*)

Elsie replaces Banquo's ghost

Elsie/Lady Macbeth Macbeth? Chuck? Are you sure you wouldn't like to go and lie down?

Norm/Macbeth Has he gone?

Elsie/Lady Macbeth There's nobody here. Look!

Norm/Macbeth There is! There is! (*He looks*) Oh ... there isn't.

Elsie/Lady Macbeth I think you're a little bit on edge, dear.

Norm/Macbeth Ay. It's kingin'. It's getting on me nerves. All this murderin' and everything—and then you can't even be sure they're going to stay dead when you've killed 'em! It's drivin' me up the wall. It were that bleedin' Witch as started it. I've a good mind to go round and see her tomorrow, give her a piece of my mind.

Elsie/Lady Macbeth But you don't know where she lives. Don't get yourself so worked up.

Norm/Macbeth It'll be in Yellow Pages. I'll find her. Then there's Macduff. What's he up to? Not turnin' up for Royal banquet, leavin' trumped-up excuses. I don't like it. 'E's up to no good, the jumped-up little ... Plottin'! I bet that's what he's doin'! Conspirin'! But what? What? I tell you, it's starting to prey on me mind. (*He narrows his eyes*) You're even starting to look like bloody Macduff! Aaaagh!

Elsie/Lady Macbeth Calm down, calm down! You'll get ulcers if you carry on like this. It's a nice cup of Horlicks and beddy-byes for you, my lad.

Norm/Macbeth   Strange things I have in head that will to hand,
                          Which must be acted ere they may be scanned.

Elsie/Lady Macbeth You lack the season of all natures, sleep.

Lady Macbeth exits

Norm/Macbeth   Come, we'll to sleep. My strange and self abuse
                          Is the initiate fear that wants hard use.
                          We are yet but young in deed.

He makes to exit, pauses and turns in the doorway

Norm "Strange and self abuse!" Do they let schoolkids read this stuff? Honestly, that William!

Norm exits

Elsie enters as the Witch

Elsie/Witch Ha haaaa! Yes, it's me again, everybody, the flying sorceress! (*Cackle*)

                          Macbeth's coming round in a minute or two
                          To have his fortune read.
                          He doesn't know what the 'ell to do
                          Since he cut off Duncan's head.
                          He can't see that he's buggered things up,
                          And he's going to come a cropper—
                          So I'll give him some cryptic prophecies
                          And mess his mind up proper! (*Cackle*)

Elsie Now there's supposed to be a Witches' song here, according to William. Typical William, of course, doesn't say what song it's supposed to be. Never mind, though, 'cos I've chosen one suitable. Here we go.

She strikes a pose, then breaks into a tap-dance routine, while singing "That Old Black Magic". This is a full-scale show-stopper, and Elsie gives it the works: pseudo-Shirley Bassey vocal trills, plenty of wiggling and grand gestures, etc. She makes up to a gentleman in the audience, sitting on his knee and kissing him. Big finish. Riotous applause, Elsie kissing her hands to the audience

Norman enters as Macbeth

Norm/Macbeth How now, you secret, black and midnight hag!

Elsie/Witch Hallo, Macbeth. It's taken you long enough to get here. Bus break down, did it? (*Cackle*)

Norm/Macbeth Very amusin'. You would have to have an ex-directory lair. It's taken me all day tryin' to find this place in the Witchfinder A to Z. Worn out, I am.

Elsie/Witch Well, anything I can do for you, now you're here? As if I didn't know! (*Cackle*)

Norm/Macbeth It's about them prophecies that you did—you know, about me bein' King and everything? Well, they seem to have worked out all right, and I want some more, OK?

Elsie/Witch Well, you've come to the right place. Grizelda Crone, clairvoyant extraordinaire! Palms read, future foreseen, questions answered— small, large, and——

Norm/Macbeth Don't say it!

Elsie/Witch —medium! (*Cackle, cackle, cackle*)

Macbeth groans in pain at this appalling joke

I presume you'll be wantin' to commune directly with the Great Spirits on the etheric plane, won't you? So that'll be twelve pounds seventy-five plus VAT, including any spells and potions. Now let's see, where's my *Reader's Digest Witch's Handy Book of Spells*? (*She gets it from the shelf*) Now, what exactly was it you wanted to know?

Norm/Macbeth (*airily*) Oh, you know, usual sort of stuff. Who to beware of, how to stay King forever and that. Derby winner'd be useful, too, if you could manage it.

Elsie/Witch Horses isn't my line, love. You want a veterinary witch for that. Now, let's see, it'll be under Prophecies, Royal, General Purposes . . . Ah! Here we are! I thought so. We'll be needing a potion. I'll just get the oven warmed up.

Norm/Macbeth Just a minute. Aren't you supposed to have a cauldron and a fire, and stuff?

Elsie/Witch Oh no, dear. Ever so messy, that sort of thing. Them cauldrons are a bugger to wash up. I'll do it in me Pyrex casserole. Now then. (*She gets out the casserole, and the ingredients for the potion, which are all in appropriately labelled packets and bottles*)

> Powdered batswing, a teaspoonful,
> An ounce of lizard paste,
> Some dehydrated toadstools,
> And viper's dung, to taste.

She tastes it. Mmmm!

Two or three dead babies' fingers
According to the weight,
With a dash of permitted flavouring
And monosodium glutamate.

A leper's toenail, finely ground,
With a measure of Campari,
A couple of warts, some HP sauce,
And tamari, and tamari, and tamari.

Put it on the bottom shelf
In a low to moderate oven,
Say a black mass twice a day
And support your local coven! (*Cackle*)
There! That should do it! Fag? (*She offers him one*)

Norm/Macbeth Er, no ta. (*He looks round apprehensively*) Well, what happens now, then? Where's the ghostly apparitions? Where's the knockin' on the table and that? Isn't the room supposed to fill up with Elastoplast?

Elsie/Witch Ectoplasm. No, love. Don't get yourself all excited. You shouldn't believe everything you read in the *News of the World*. Here, switch the wireless on—you might get some results soon. (*Cackle*)

She passes Macbeth a portable radio from the sideboard. He looks doubtful, but switches it on

Radio ... Alloa Athletic two, Dundee three; Glasgow Celtic four, Motherwell nil; Forfar Athletic three, Hamilton Academicals two; Airdrionians two——

Norm/Macbeth Highly amusin'! Very funny! If that's your idea of results ...

Elsie/Witch Keep listenin'!

Radio —Hibernians nil, Macbeth beware Macduff; Aberdeen two——

Norm/Macbeth (*switching the radio off*) I knew it! I knew it! That bastard, Macduff! Oh, I should have had him done in! He keeps appearin' in me dreams all the time. Everybody's startin' to look like him! (*He narrows his eyes*) Come to think of it, you look a lot like him! Aaagh!

Elsie/Witch Calm down, calm down! We've not finished yet. (*She switches the radio on*)

Radio ... And now, from all at Number sixty-four, this is for Lance-Corporal Bill Jenkins in BFPO forty-one and Doreen says——

The Witch exits, unnoticed by Macbeth

—"Please listen to the words, Bill, and remember it won't be long till Easter"——Be lion-mettled, proud, and take no care who chafes, who frets, or where conspirers are. Macbeth shall never vanquished be until great Birnam Wood to high Dunsinane Hill shall come against him.

Music: something sickly by Jim Reeves or similar

Norm/Macbeth Great! Smashin'! Birnam Wood's not going to be moving, is it? Not likely! Mind you, I think I'll have the Forestry Commission executed, just in case. Looks like there's plenty more reignin' to do. Best be having a palace designed. And see to that Macduff.

The music stops

Radio We interrupt this programme to broadcast a message for a Mr Macbeth, occupation King, last seen near Dunsinane, Scotland: "Be bloody, bold, and resolute; laugh to scorn the power of man, for none of woman born shall harm Macbeth."

Norm/Macbeth (*switching the radio off*) No man born of woman, eh? Safe! Home and dry! Just let that Macduff try it on now! Or anybody! I mean, every bugger's born of woman, aren't they? (*Sudden doubt*) Unless that gooseberry bush stuff me mum told me really is true. No. Ha-haaa! (*He punches the air, like a victorious footballer*) Is that it, then? Any more prophesyin'? (*Turning*) Mrs Witch? Where's she gone? Bloody hell, vanished! Still, I suppose witches do a lot of that sort of stuff, don't they? Anyway, she's gone without giving me the bill.

Elsie enters as the Messenger

Elsie/Messenger Mr Macbeth?

Norm/Macbeth King Macbeth to you, mate.

Elsie/Messenger (*shrugging*) Have it your own way. I've got a telegram for you from England.

Norm/Macbeth Another telegram! I've never had so many telegrams since I started this kingin' lark. Is it a singing telegram? I've always wanted one of them.

Elsie/Messenger No it isn't.

Norm/Macbeth No it isn't, *My Liege*! Just remember who's King round here! Let's have some bleedin' respect! I'm the King, understand, and if I say I want a singing telegram, I get a singing telegram, all right? And kneel while you're at it!

Elsie/Messenger (*kneeling*) OK, my Liege. (*Singing very badly and loudly*)
I think that you're a rotten King.
I've had about enough.
I've run away to England,
So up yours, signed Macduff.

The Messenger exits

Norm/Macbeth Run away to England, has he? Right then, best be murderin' his family! Mac-bloody-duff! (*Sudden panic. He looks back at the door where the Messenger just left*) You know, that messenger looked a bit like him, as well! I think I'm going out of me mind! (*He blows his whistle. No response. He blows it again. Calling*) Murderer! ... Oi, Murderer! ... You can never find one when you want one!

Macbeth exits

Elsie enters as Lady Macduff. She hangs a large card saying "Macduff Mansions" on the wall. She is wearing another housecoat in another tartan, and a hairnet. She speaks in a pseudo-posh Edinburgh accent, VERY fast

Elsie/Lady Macduff Gone off to England, has he? Fancy that. Daft bugger, he's probably sucking up to that Prince Malcolm. What's the point of that, I ask you? It's Macbeth he should be buttering up. It's Macbeth who's King, after all. He'll not get promotion that way. He's probably only done it to get out of painting the loft. Said he was going to do it this weekend before my mother came to stay. Men! And here I am, a poor helpless woman left alone to fend for herself, with only her little son to look after her. And where is he? Why isn't he looking after his old mother in her time of need? Jimmy! *Jimmy!*

She goes off, and comes straight back on with a life-size stuffed dummy, dressed as a schoolboy. She sits it in a chair

Now then Jimmy, look lively! Straighten your tie, will you, you look a right mess! I don't know what's the matter with you. Have you been smoking that funny haggis again? Now shut up, will you, and listen! Your father's gone away to England, so you're the man of the house now; so, first thing I want that lawn mowed, then there's that shelf in the kitchen needs fixing—the garage needs a coat of paint as well—what? Stop interrupting, will you! (*She hits him*) Where was I? You've broken my train of thought, aggravating little devil! (*She hits him*) Honestly, I don't know what I've done wrong to deserve a son like you. Me and your dad have worked our fingers to the bone—well, we've worked the servants' fingers to the bone, anyway—to give you a nice castle to live in, and what do we get? And that's enough of your lip! Cheeky young devil! (*She hits him*) Now then, as temporary head of the household, it's time you started showing a bit of responsibility. *And sit up straight!* (*She sits him up and hits him*) And you haven't combed your hair, have you? (*She hits him*) Honestly, you're a disgrace, you are. To think that the noble name of Macduff has got to be carried on by you after your dear father passes on! It makes me weep, it really does! And shut up, will you! (*She hits him*) Honestly, I can't get a word in edgeways with all your backchat! Ungrateful little bugger! (*She knocks a teacup off the table*) Now look what you've made me do! That's coming out of your pocket money, my lad! (*She hits him*) Making me smash up the priceless Macduff family porcelain, you vandal! (*She knocks him out of the chair*) You nasty little brat! (*She smashes his head on the floor*) Take that! (*She kicks him*) And that! (*She kicks him, takes him by the leg and whirls him round her head, smashes him to the floor, jumps up and down on him*) And just you wait till your father gets home!

Norman enters as the Murderer

Norm/Murderer 'Ullo.

Elsie/Lady Macduff Who the hell are you? What d'you mean by barging in here without so much as a by-your-leave? Why didn't you use the tradesmen's entrance? Well?

Norm/Murderer Er . . . sorry.

Elsie/Lady Macduff Well, what do you want?

Norm/Murderer I come ter kill you.

Elsie/Lady Macduff (*screaming*) Aaaaagh! Oh, what's to become of us? Jimmy! Do something! See him off! Defend your poor old mother that loves you! Don't lie there like a dummy! (*To the Murderer*) Whatever do you want to do such a terrible thing to us for?

Norm/Murderer It's 'cos you bin bad. (*He produces a gun*)

Elsie/Lady Macduff (*screaming*) Aaaaagh! But you can't! You can't! You can't just shoot a poor defenceless mother and her doting son like that, in cold blood! You can't!

Norm/Murderer (*puzzled*) Oh . . .

Pause, then he empties the gun at them. Lady Macduff keels over, screaming, and "dies". The Murderer looks down at them, then up, knowingly, at the audience

I *knew* she was wrong about that!

The Murderer exits

Elsie gets to her feet

Elsie Now, don't get excited everybody! You see, I'm not really dead. It's still me, Elsie Grimethorpe! I just thought I'd remind you that it's only a play, being as how it's getting so violent. I bet you were getting carried away, weren't you? It's very dramatic, isn't it? Course it is! But just remember it's only me and Norman, 'cos we wouldn't like anybody that's of a nervous disposition havin' a Cadillac arrest or anything, would we, Norman?

Norm (*off*) What?

Elsie I'm just sayin' about how we don't want anyone havin' a heart attack, what with the vividly re-created scenes of violence and brutality what we are presentin'.

Norm (*off*) Oh ay.

Elsie I'm very sorry about the violence and brutality, by the way, everybody, but I'm afraid it's that sort of play—and we all know who to blame for that, don't we? Yes! Well, you have been warned. Next scene: England, at the court of King Edward.

Elsie exits with the dummy

Norman enters as Malcolm. He is wearing short trousers

Norm/Malcolm Cor! It's great wearin' proper trousers! They got pockets in what you can put things in. And you can put your hands in your pockets, too. Mind you, soon as you do, all them smelly courtiers start tellin' you to take your hands out of your pockets in front of the King! Honest, it's nearly as bad as school, sometimes, is court! I keep tellin' 'em I'm a king too, or at least I would be if it wasn't for smelly horrible Macbeth, but they never take any notice, rotten pigs! Not that their measly old King Edward's anything to write home about. He's bats as a coot, he is! I tell you what—I smashed a window in the palace toilets this morning, playing Hereward the Wake, and one of them courtiers was going to smash me up for it, so I said, "I never done it!" and King Edward said, "That's right, he never, 'cos *I* done it!" And then he said he wrote "The Venerable Bede is a

boring old fart" on the palace wall—and he never, 'cos I done it! And
then he said he done the Great Train Robbery, and sunk the *Titanic*, and
all sorts of other stuff as well. And all them poncy courtiers just smiled
and said, "Yes, Sire." Seems like he's always doing it. Confesses to
everything. I'm surprised he ever gets any kingin' done at all. He's just all
the time confessin'! Catch me doing that when I'm the King!

Elsie enters as Macduff

Elsie/Macduff My Liege!

Norm/Malcolm Coo! It's Macduff! I thought you was in Scotland, cour-
tierin' at Macbeth's. What you doin' here?

Elsie/Macduff My Liege, I am come to beg you to return to Scotland. Your
country is in sore need of you.

Norm/Malcolm What? Go back? And have to go to that rotten smelly
school again? And get bashed up by big horrible Macbeth, as like as not.
Not likely! I like it here.

Elsie/Macduff But, Sire, you are the rightful heir to the throne. Scotland
groans beneath the tyrannical heel of Macbeth. The whole economy's
going to rack and ruin because of his mad schemes! He's got some sort of
bee in his bonnet about trees—he had the Forestry Commission executed
and put out a reward for every tree anyone cut down. There are posters up
all over the kingdom saying, "Use More Wood, especially Birnam
Wood!" What can it mean? He's even trying to force people to wear
wooden kilts! He's also keeping a twenty-four-hour watch on maternity
hospitals, to make sure that only women have babies! Why? It's bank-
rupting the treasury! He's had to devalue the groat! Sire, you must return,
if only out of concern for your subjects.

Norm/Malcolm I knew school would come into it somewhere! Well, I don't
want any rotten subjects! I hate subjects! I've decided to not ever do any
subjects ever again, so there!

Elsie/Macduff Sire, you misunderstand. You must return to Scotland to
take your rightful place as King.

Norm/Malcolm King?

Elsie/Macduff King.

Norm/Malcolm An' rule, an' make laws and that?

Elsie/Macduff Of course.

Norm/Malcolm Cor! Great! I'll make Scotland a really smashing country, I
will! I'll close all the schools, and make parents illegal. Yeah! And cover
the whole country with Scalextric! And nobody over fourteen's going to
have the vote!

Elsie/Macduff Sire, no-one has a vote anyway. Scotland is a monarchy.

Norm/Malcolm Well, nobody's going to have the vote, then, *specially*
anybody over fourteen! And I'll have an Olympic BMX team, and make
Smarties free, and abolish soppy girls! Well . . . except for playing Doctors
and Nurses with. Fantastic! I can hardly wait!

Elsie/Macduff (*aside*) I wonder if I'm doing the right thing.

Norm/Malcolm 'Ere, but what about Macbeth, though? What we going to
do about him?

Elsie/Macduff I thought perhaps King Edward might help you out. Perhaps
you could have a quiet word with him, you know, King to King.

Norm/Malcolm Yeah. Good idea!

He runs off, calling, "King Edward! Ted! Teddy!"

Elsie/Macduff   The noble Malcolm, Prince of Scots
                                  Shall save our country now
                                  From Macbeth's dark and evil plots,
                                  Though I really don't see how.

Norm enters as the Messenger

Norm/Messenger You Mr Macduff?

Elsie/Macduff That's right.

Norm/Messenger I gotta message for you from Scotland.

Elsie/Macduff It's not one of those singing telegrams, is it?

Norm/Messenger Course not.

Elsie/Macduff Does it rhyme?

Norm/Messenger No.

Elsie/Macduff Thank God for that! What does it say?

Norm/Messenger It's from Macbeth. It says, "Have murdered your wife——

Elsie/Macduff I knew he couldn't be all bad.

Norm/Messenger —and family. Also dug up your allotment and turned your castle into bijou Highland holiday flatlets. Hoping this finds you as it leaves me, yours Macbeth (King). PS. Ha ha!"

Elsie/Macduff The swine! He's gone too far this time! My prize shallots, gone! I'll make him pay for this! (*He goes to the door and calls*) Malcolm! Sire!

Pause. He calls again, more emphatically. He looks pointedly at Norman. The penny drops

Norman looks aghast and rushes off, tearing off his Messenger costume. He re-enters immediately, scrambling into his Malcolm costume

Norm/Malcolm ... And maybe we could have marbles instead of money. And nationalize jelly babies. Cor! I got lots of ideas!

Elsie/Macduff Well? Did you parley with the King, my Liege?

Norm/Malcolm What? Oh, yeah.

Elsie/Macduff And?

Norm/Malcolm Well, after he'd confessed to murderin' Christ and sinkin' Atlantis, and one or two other things, he said he'd be glad to lend me a few thousand soldiers to go and smash up Macbeth. He said it was part of his community policing policy, or something ...

Elsie/Macduff Onwards, then! And death to Macbeth!

Norm/Malcolm Yeah! We'll smash him to bits with supersonic planes and tanks and atomic warheads and Cruise missiles and laser beams——

Elsie/Macduff Hardly likely, Sire; this is only the eleventh century. We've barely invented the bow and arrow yet.

Macduff exits

Norm/Malcolm (*crestfallen*) Oh. (*Then, perking up, he sings*) Da dah da diddley dah da daaah! (*To the tune of the "Robin Hood" theme of the 1960s. He exits, pretending he's shooting a bow and arrow, and saying loudly*) Twanggg! Twanggg!

Malcolm exits

Norm (*off*) Next scene: back in Scotland, at Macbeth's castle at Dunsinane.

Elsie enters as Lady Macbeth, "sleepwalking". She wears a nightie, and carries a toy dog under her arm. The dog's "barking" is done by Norman, from off stage

Elsie/Lady Macbeth Ooooooooh! All them sleeping pills! Ooooooooh! I wish I could wake up! Ooooooooooh! Poor old Duncan!

Woof!

Ooooooooh! Poor old Banquo!

Woof, woof!

Ooooooooh! Poor me!

Woof, woof, woof!

I'm fed up being Royal! All that blood, and death, and murder and everything! Ooooooooooh! And I can't stand the smell of that Arabian perfume! Ooooooooh! I wish I'd never started it all now! Ooooooooh! Ooooooooooh!

She continues moaning; the "dog" joins in, howling; the noise reaches a crescendo, till she hits the dog round the head and hurls it off stage

Out, damned Spot!

> I think I'll go and hang myself, now,
> From the upstairs rafter.
> Don't tell Macbeth I've done it, though—
> I should have died here, after.

Lady Macbeth exits

Norman enters as Macbeth. He is very jumpy, and constantly looks behind him. He circles a houseplant warily, waving his sword at it

Norm/Macbeth Is it going to move? It better not, that's all! Trees! They're everywhere, always looking at you, waiting to pounce! Ha! (*He whirls round to confront another houseplant*) Thought you had me there, didn't you, nasty little green get! (*To the audience, from front stage*) God, I'm fed up with this lark! I never thought kingin' was going to be as bad as this! Everybody's out to get me. Malcolm and Macduff have come back from England now—and I bet it's not to take me out for a pint. I've a good mind to pack it all in and go and seek political asylum. Somewhere nice and quiet. Beirut, maybe. (*Or whichever trouble spot is in the news this week*)

During this speech, Macduff enters, also carrying a sword. He moves stealthily towards Macbeth, pushing in front of him a houseplant on a small side-table on castors, as "camouflage"

Macbeth finally notices the "moving" plant

AAAAAAAAAAAAAGH! It's moving! It's moving!

He cowers behind the sofa, sobbing, until Macduff comes out from behind the plant

Oh, it's you, Macduff! (*He gets up*) What do you want to play about like that for? I thought you were a tree moving around for a minute, there. Well? Come back to say you're sorry, have you?

Elsie/Macduff Foul recreant! I am come to take from thee that crown which thou hast usurped, and return it to its rightful heir—Malcolm, Prince of Scotland!

Norm/Macbeth That spotty little brat! Give over, will you! And stop waving that sword around. No man what is born of woman can hurt me, and I've had that said in a proper prophecy, so sling it! You're not frightening me!

Elsie/Macduff Prepare to meet thine end, vile canker! For truly, Macduff is no man born of woman!

Norm/Macbeth Not a man born of woman? Where did you come from, then, out of a test-tube? Actually, looking at you I wouldn't be at all surprised. (*He snickers*)

Elsie/Macduff I'm not a man born of woman, yer big chuff! I'm not a man! See? (*He opens his jacket to reveal the shape of breasts*)

Norm/Macbeth Oh all right, then! Have the bleedin' crown! (*He hurls it at him*) I give up! I'm sick to death of kingin' anyway! It's not what it's cracked up to be, I tell you! All that murderin', and ghosts comin' after you, and trees walking about! (*He trips over his "royal robe"*) And always fallin' over your royal robe! (*He takes it off, and hurls it at Macduff*) Here, take it! I don't want it! I've had enough!

Elsie/Macduff Now die, villain!

Norm/Macbeth Oh, lay off, Macduff!

Macduff leaps on him, brandishing his sword, and knocks him over on to the sofa. They wrestle

Norm For God's sake! What you doin'? Stop it! Give over! Macduff! Elsie! Pack it in! What're you trying to do?

Elsie I'm trying to cut your head off, love.

Norm Cut me head off? Don't be so bloody daft! What for?

Elsie I've got to, love. It says so in the play.

Norm Says so? Says so? Who says so?

Elsie Shakespeare says so.

Norm What, Arnold?

Elsie No, WILLIAM! (*She lunges*)

Norm (*extricating himself and standing up quickly so that the lunge misses*) Right! This has gone far enough I'm not standing for no more! Bloody William! (*Calling*) William!

William enters. He wears a grubby boiler suit, and a big collar and bald-head wig à la Shakespeare

William Yes?

Norm Look, lad. I don't know how to break this to you, but I don't think you're cut out for play-writing. You're no good at it. If you take my advice, you'll go into scrap-dealin', like your dad. Leave playwriting to other people. Go on, run along.

William makes to leave, crestfallen

Oh, and you can tell Arnold we'll be going for a pint later on, if he's interested.

William exits

(*To Elsie*) Come on, love, get your coat on. I'll buy you a port and lemon. (*He starts changing back into his own clothes*)

Elsie (*changing, and getting her coat*) Well, everybody, I hope you all enjoyed this little bit of culture. It were very nice to see you. Mind you, I think we'll be going back to Trivial Pursuit in future, somehow. Now, don't forget to turn the lights off, will you, when you go.

Norm (*grabbing her arm and pulling her to the door*) Come on, then, woman! They don't stay open all night!

They wave to the audience from the doorway

Elsie   ⎫
       ⎬ (*together*) Good-night!
Norm   ⎭

They exit

CURTAIN

FURNITURE AND PROPERTY LIST

ACT I

On stage: *Kitchen area:*
Cooker
Sink
Kitchen units. *On one:* glass, bottle of Domestos

Living area:
Sofa
Armchairs
Sideboard. *In it:* stick of dynamite, large cigarette paper, cigarette lighter, radio
Dining-table. *On it:* paper and pencil
Bookshelves. *On one:* "Book of Spells"
Picture of Prince Charles and Princess Di on wall
Several large houseplants
Various ornaments
Copy of *Macbeth* for **Elsie**
Kilt with braces, tin hat, toy sword for **Norman**

Off stage: *Costumes and props required:*
Crown, false moustache, plaid car blanket **(Elsie/Duncan)**
Pointy black hat, vacuum cleaner **(Elsie/Witch)**
Tartan jacket, tam-o'-shanter, Banquo—large toy panda with kilt **(Norm/Macbeth)**
Postman's hat, glasses, false nose and moustache set, clipboard, pencil, postbag containing brown paper parcel **(Elsie/Messenger)**
Tartan housecoat, postcard **(Elsie/Lady Macbeth)**
Postman's hat, glasses, false nose and moustache set, telegram **(Norm/Messenger)**
Tartan jacket, tam-o'-shanter **(Norm/Macbeth)**
Crown, false moustache, plaid car blanket **(Elsie/Duncan)**
Tartan housecoat **(Elsie/Lady Macbeth)**
Dead chicken **(Norm/Macbeth)**
Tartan housecoat, Banquo, Fleance—smaller toy panda in kilt, doll dressed as Malcolm and hat pin in pocket **(Elsie/Lady Macbeth)**
School blazer, cap, kilt, "tadpoles" **(Norm/Malcolm)**
False beard, tweed jacket, deerstalker hat, pipe **(Elsie/Macduff)**
School blazer, cap, kilt **(Norm/Malcolm)**
False beard, tweed jacket, deerstalker hat, pipe, Banquo **(Elsie/Macduff)**
Tartan jacket, tam-o'-shanter, large knife **(Norm/Macbeth)**
Tartan jacket, crown, plaid car blanket, police whistle around neck **(Norm/Macbeth)**
Black mask, black and red striped jumper **(Elsie/Murderer)**
Tartan housecoat **(Elsie/Lady Macbeth)**
Banquo, Fleance **(Norman)**
Black mask, black and red striped jumper, gun **(Elsie/Murderer)**
Tartan jacket, crown, plaid car blanket, whistle **(Norm/Macbeth)**

ACT II

Set: Tidy set
    On dining-table: tablecloth, cutlery, cups, saucers, party blower, bottle of
       tablets
    Under table: Banquo's ghost—panda with sheet over it
    On cooker: saucepans, one containing baked beans, spoons
    Beside cooker: two plates with toast
    On work surface: Pyrex casserole, labelled packets and bottles of ingredi-
       ents for potion, packet of cigarettes
    Behind chair: **Elsie**'s clothes and coat

Costumes: Diamante tiara, frilly nylon robe **(Elsie/Lady Macbeth)**
    Tartan jacket, crown, plaid car blanket, whistle **(Norm/Macbeth)**

Off stage: Pointy black hat **(Elsie/Witch)**
    Postman's hat, glasses, false nose and moustache set, telegram **(Elsie/**
      Messenger)
    Another tartan housecoat, hairnet, card "MACDUFF MANSIONS"
      (Elsie/Lady Macduff)
    Lifesize schoolboy dummy **(Elsie/Lady Macduff)**
    Black mask, black and red striped jumper, gun **(Norm/Murderer)**
    School blazer, cap, short trousers **(Norm/Malcolm)**
    False beard, tweed jacket, deerstalker hat, pipe **(Elsie/Macduff)**
    Postman's hat, glasses, false nose and moustache set, telegram **(Norm/**
      Messenger)
    School blazer, cap, short trousers **(Norm/Malcolm)**
    Nightie, tiara, toy dog **(Elsie/Lady Macbeth)**
    Tartan jacket, crown, plaid car blanket, sword **(Norm/Macbeth)**
    False beard, tweed jacket, deerstalker hat, pipe, sword, houseplant on
      small table on castors **(Elsie/Macduff)**

LIGHTING PLOT

Property fittings required: nil

Interior. A living-room/kitchen. The same scene throughout

ACT I Evening

To open: Black-out

Cue 1	**Norm** (*off*): "Where's me teeth?" *Bring up general interior lighting*	(Page 1)

ACT II Evening

To open: General interior lighting

No cues

EFFECTS PLOT

ACT I

Cue 1   As play begins   (Page 1)
Clap of thunder

Cue 2   **Norm/Macbeth** exits   (Page 1)
Enormous banging, crashing and shrieking, off

Cue 3   **Elsie** exits   (Page 12)
Door chimes

Cue 4   **Norm/Malcolm** exits, followed by infuriated **Elsie/Lady Mac-** (Page 15)
       beth
Huge crash off

Cue 5   **Elsie/Lady Macbeth** (*off*): "... I'll get a man in in the morn- (Page 15)
       ing."
Several loud pistol shots

Cue 6   **Elsie/Murderer** shoots Banquo   (Page 20)
Gunshot

ACT II

Cue 7   **Elsie/Witch** sings her show-stopping song   (Page 24)
Accompanying music

Cue 8   **Norm/Macbeth** switches on radio   (Page 26)
Voice from radio as text

Cue 9   **Elsie/Witch** switches on radio   (Page 26)
Voice and music from radio as text

Cue 10   **Norm/Murderer** empties gun at **Elsie/Lady Macduff** and Jimmy   (Page 29)
Gunshots

MADE AND PRINTED IN GREAT BRITAIN BY
LATIMER TREND & COMPANY LTD PLYMOUTH